The Christmas Basilica

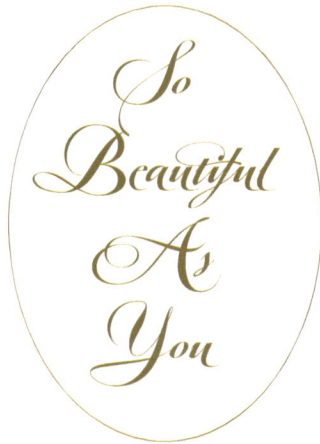

So
Beautiful
As
You

Additional Books by Dr. Ann Marie Nielsen

Holy Mother Carry Us

Diamonds of the Holy Heart

Pearls of the Presence

Father Ahavah

www.motherahavah.com/books

The Christmas Basilica

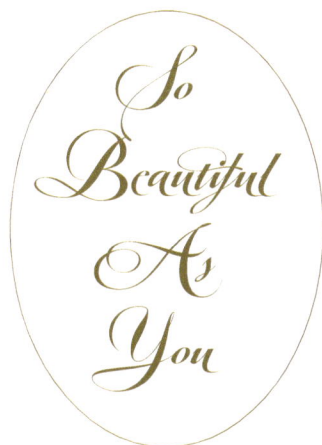

So Beautiful As You

DR. ANN MARIE NIELSEN

*t*NS

the NAMELESS
S P E A K S
PUBLICATIONS

The Christmas Basilica: So Beautiful As You

Copyright © 2017 by Dr. Ann Marie Nielsen

FIRST EDITION

ISBN-13: 978-0-9975228-5-3

ISBN-10: 0-9975228-5-2

Published by The Nameless Speaks Publications, Florida USA

Set in Tramuntana 1 Text Pro

Book design, front and back covers, page borders by Dr. Ann Marie Nielsen

www.motherahavah.com

Available worldwide from Amazon and other online and traditional book sellers.

In the *Christmas Basilica*

Of the exalted Heart

Nothing is missing

In the *Christmas Basilica*

Of the perennial Heart

There is nothing

So Beautiful

As You

In the *Christmas Basilica*

Of the immortal Heart

God Presence Is

Consciousness Is

Awareness Alighted with Love Is

The Nativity of the Free and the Tender... Is

The Noel of the Infinity of Opulence... Is

As You

Nothing so Beautiful

As You

In the *Christmas Basilica*

The secret of the *Noel-diamond-void*

Sparkles its stunning wisdoms

Of the nascent stelliform peace

That shines as ever emptied-vast

Emptied of cold worries, and mean strivings

The *Noel-Diamond-Void*

Is the bliss of the serene emptying

The emptying-absolving of adhesive stress

That reveals the clean unattached peace

Of the kingdom of thriving

Thriving happens inherently

Naturally, naturally

In unhindered flourish

In every instant

Whether the glory blooms

Are seen

Or not seen

By self-consumed eyes

That cannot see *You*

Or by eyes dimmed by the shadows

Of towering circumstance

Or by eyes strained and dismayed

By unresolved heartaches

Still...still

In the inherent rhythms of Light

Right here now

Celestial thriving Is

The sweet nectar of Love Is

As You

The flourish

Of the *Christmas Basilica*

Ecstatically airbrushes high glory

The brilliant thrill of *The Quieting*

The Primordial Hush of breathtaking beauty

In every second

Of every scene

In the *Noel-Diamond-Void*

Limits empty to zero point

Limitlessness dawns in soft frosted dazzle shine

As every fear, heavy with condensation

As every limitation, laden with dull constraint

Empties to a *heaven-spun infinity dot*

The remembrance of the dot happens...

Happens!

That dot of golden Light

The Essence of Presence

Is the whole of Infinity

Not the Infinity of stuff or things

Not the Infinity of ten thousand things

That falter, fade, or fall away

The Real Infinity

Love, unconditioned

Love unconditional

You

The beauty

That *Diamond Dot*

Of Gold Presence Light

Is the Holy Joy

The Borderless Silence

The Stardust Immortal Beauty

From that *Diamond Dot*

Any glorious universe can form

Of breathtaking wonderment

In cacophonies of resounding Life

Chorusing:

Nothing so Beautiful as You

That Sound

That Sound...

...And its Knowingness

Sparks the light formation

Of heaven-worlds created

Of heart-worlds painted-legitimized

Victoriousness Is

Kingdoms, Queendoms of God

Orchestrated, populated

At the mere divine pulse-thought of them

From that *Adamantine Dot*

The Adamantine Dot of You

As Infinity-Love-Awareness

A global sweetness dawns

An infinite realm

Streaming... without... moving

Noble, avid joy of bounteous creation

Right in the midst...right in the very midst...

Of what seems stalled in the finite

In the old abject hurting

Or what seems frozen in lack,

Stuck in time—

Solid like ice...

Staring there...

Staring back...

Until the Adamantine Dot

The Adamantine Golden-Infinite Dot of You

Of indestructible warm Light and Sound

Kindles the crystalline hum

Right in the center

Of even the most icy-seeming trial or experience

Revealing the true resounding Light hum

As the real essence of symphonies of harmony

Right where the clanging icy ordeal
Used to congeal and repeat...again

The Adamantine Dot
Opens as the whole of Infinity
As rhythms of Light
Lullabies of kind reverence
Melting away all forlorn pain
Forever

Hallelujah

Ever instantaneous
Ascendent joy upon joy
The Christmas Way
The Christmas Basilica
Of gentle merriment
Kind mysteries
Enchanted magicalness
And reverent holiness

From that *Diamond Dot*

Which is the whole of the

Tangible-infinite-realness

An altar of unification forms

This Christmas englobed altar

Weds-unifies

The bonds of ecstatic friendship

Kindred spirits greet the light

Diamond Dot sees the Diamond Dot

Everywhere

Diamond Dot Consciousness-Love

Aware of Diamond Dot Consciousness-Love

The Vision

Illuminating the landscapes

As vivid heavenscapes

Right in the midst of the now-fading

Foggy land perceptions of vague-old appearances

Hallelujah

The Christmas Basilica

In a shared symphony of knowing

Hearts resound

Round and round

In choruses of:

I have never seen

Anything

So Beautiful

As You

Hearts translucent

Hearts sculptured free of iron dross

Every rigidity now hushed and beveled

With the kind chisels of compassion

To reveal the blinding Light

Of the Noel of Compassion

The Christmas Basilica

Christ is born

Means The God of Compassion

Reveals in all hearts

That there is no death...

That there is no disappointment

Which is another form of death...

Resurrection breathes every expression

Resurrection makes every grave of old pain

The Love Gaze of God

Holding you close and high

And intimately known

As Itself

Eternal intimate face to face Love

Breath to breath Love

Gaze to Gaze Love

The Christmas Basilica

The Christmas Basilica

The Christmas Noel

Of being emptied of all death

By seeing the Original Dot

Of Original Life

In all that seemed like death

Nothing

So Beautiful

As You

Resurrection Is

Life Is

The Christmas Basilica

Immortal Joy

The Golden Diamond Castle

Of the Diamond of Consciousness

Of the Realness Self

Shines as Beauty

Aware of

Beholding Beauty

The Christmas Instant

Alive as That

Christmas has no lack

No want

No hurt

In the Noel of Compassion

So Beautiful

As You

Lack, want, and hurt

Come home to nurture-land

In the vast, verdant, starlit

Gardenscapes of *Compassion*

And fade into nativities of opulence

Ever pulsing

Not ever leaving

Cared for

Carried

Alive as the Caring-ness

Compassion Is

Consciousness Is

Carried as Consciousness:

Compassion's Vision

The christened chorus resounds

Like a halo of coronation around you

A temple of goodness within you

As you hear

And feel

All of Heaven

And Heaven's Creator

Intone:

So Beautiful

As You

In the *Christmas Basilica*

The wisdom alights

That makes

So Beautiful as You

True...true...

Beauty-Innocence

The Light of True Identity

Beauty-Infinity

The Light of True Identity

Beauty-Love

The Light of True Identity

Beauty-Limitlessness

The Light of True Identity

The Heart of the Voice

In the *Christmas Basilica*

Ceaselessly sings to our Origin

Our Beloved Creator:

I have never seen

Anything so Beautiful

As You

In being the Beauty of Spirit

One moment you behold

And see...

A new era arises

The human being...

Animates

Like a moving mirror image

Reflecting in every nuance and movement

The unmoving Eternal Beauty

The beauty of holiness

The beauty of grace

The beauty of peace

The beauty of exquisite balance

And supreme wholeness

I have never seen

Anything

So Beautiful

As You

The symphony of the Song Gaze

God's Love Gaze

Beholding

You

Singing, singing over you....

So Beautiful

As You

Alive as the eternal beauty

Seeing every being

As. . . ever as. . .

So Beautiful

In the Christmas Basilica

One instant of feeling

That holy immensity

Of ineffable Love

And all shadows of separation

Evaporate in the Light

Of 10,000 suns

Genuflecting in joy

In the beauty of Oneness

So Beautiful as You

All the Aeons of Creation

Elegantly avowing

Bearing witness:

So Beautiful

As You

In the Christmas Basilica

The awakening of Love

Dawns and *dawns*

Finality ever dawning. . .

Seeing the beauty of the Holy One

Seeing the *Holy One Gaze You*

As that beauty

Seeing all as that beauty

So Beautiful as You

I love you

Means

I behold you as *Eternal Beauty*—

The Light of Consciousness

The Heart of God Presence

The Original Self

I love you eternally means

I see the beauty of you eternally

I see the changeless "I Am" Presence

As You

You:

A vast-immortal, exquisite-miraculous

Universe of beauty

Beyond all name and form

Beyond all fixation and grasping

Beyond all images and limits

Beyond all hard aggressions

The Soft

And the Free

Beauty

As individualized Essence

The Eternal Christmas

Alive as each dancing instant

The Christmas Basilica

Awake Now

As the Evergreen Immortal Noel

The timeless Christmas

Embraced in

The Messiah

Nothing so Beautiful as You

The Jewel of Compassion

Feeling the Gaze

Of the empty-yet-full

Chalice gaze

Of the Christed Light

The Diamond Dot...

Emptied-illumined to that Dot

That liberates the world

From death

And from all sufferings —

Which are all forms of disguised death

Life Is

The Christmas Basilica

The temple of Resurrection Life

Is the Resurrection

Of the Primordial Instant

The Original moment:

Created as reverence,

So Beautiful as You

The Nativity of tenderness and wisdom

The Gold of the heart of Love

The frankincense of Original Reverence

The myrrh of purification: Original Innocence

The wise men

Serving the nativity

Beholding the whole of

Infinite beauty

At every point of itself

At the same time

As the same time

The same timeless Now

Mary Ma

Of the Vessel of Life

Origin-ing You

As Immaculate Beauty

Papa Dios

Father Ahavah

Father God

Blessing You

As the Anointed Beauty

Mother Father God

All the wise ones

Beholding You

So Beautiful as You

Ecstatically feel

Simply, quietly, know

And Know...

The beauty essence of You

Is the beauty of Creator

The beauty in all things... all beings

That Diamond Dot...

The entry way of infinity

The Diamond of Consciousness

The Christmas Love

Of the Aglow Immortal Ones

The Golden Universe

Of God *Is*

Beauty Is

Come now

Now

See. . . know. . . Know

Still in the Christmas Basilica

Still There

Here, Now

So Beautiful as You

The Christmas Basilica

Selah, Amen, Selah

www.ingramcontent.com/pod-product-compliance
Lightning Source LLC
Chambersburg PA
CBHW041756050426
42443CB00023B/18